Memories of Cabot Cove

ON LOCATION IN MENDOCINO WITH

MURDER, SHE WROTE

BARBARA REED

INTRODUCTION BY JAIN LEMOS

PARKER
—
MILLS
PRESS

To my Monte,
without him, there would be no Hill House;
and to Toni Lemos,
who made living in Mendocino interesting and fun.

Memories of Cabot Cove: On Location in Mendocino with Murder, She Wrote

© 2023 Barbara Reed

All rights reserved. No part of this book may be reproduced in whole or in part, stored in a retrieval system, or transmitted in any form, or by any means, electronic, mechanical, photocopying, recording, or otherwise, without prior permission of the author, except in the case of brief quotations embodied in critical articles or reviews.

ISBN: 979-8-9879768-1-4

First Edition April 2023
Published in the United States

Cover and interior photographs © Barbara Reed.
Introduction © Jain Lemos.
Title font Lansbury by Andreas Höfeld/FontGrube AH.
Book packaging by Parker-Mills Press.
To reach the authors, write to memories@parker-mills.com.

The information in this book is drawn from a variety of public and private sources. People depicted were photographed in public places and with their permission when possible.

Murder, She Wrote season and episode numbers mentioned in this book follow the numbering used on IMDb, the most authoritative source for information on movies, television shows, and celebrities.
Please visit imdb.com/title/tt0086765/episodes for the complete series list.

Contents

- 5   Introduction
- 10   Photo Memories
- 31   Location Call Sheet
- 42   Episodes Filmed in Mendocino
- 43   Reruns of *Murder, She Wrote*
- 44   Cabot Cove ~ Mendocino Map

Angela Lansbury filming on Lansing Street. Her love and appreciation for Mendocino are clear in her comments about the town's natural beauty, its sense of history and community, and her joy in working here.

Introduction

WHEN PEOPLE ASK WHERE I'M FROM, I sometimes describe Mendocino as the town from *Murder, She Wrote*, with a further explanation that I grew up in Northern California... not Maine. The show's creators were looking for a picturesque coastal town with that special, small-town feel. Mendocino, featuring charming Victorian homes, dramatic seascapes, fishing atmospheres, and giant forests, fit their bill perfectly as a backdrop for unraveling all sorts of mysteries.

Mendocino was already a desirable filming location in the 1980s when the producers decided to settle here. Some recognizable movies shot around town include *East of Eden* (1955), *The Russians Are Coming, the Russians Are Coming* (1966), and *Same Time, Next Year* (1978). There were a few forgettable films made, too, such as *The Dunwich Horror* (1970) and *Dead & Buried* (1981). Add *Summer of '42* (1971), *Cujo* (1983), and *Racing with the Moon* (1984) to understand the range of Hollywood power players who found their way up to us in the land of tall trees. But it was *Murder, She Wrote* who truly adopted us as a town.

Finding a setting as unique as Mendocino with relative proximity to Hollywood, about 550 miles north, made it somewhat convenient to film on location without the need for much travel or coordination; at least not to my way of thinking. The trip, which I've made too many times to count, takes nine hours by car—and that's pushing it on the I-5 with Indy-style pit stops. For *Murder, She Wrote*, above-the-line cast and crew members typically flew into San Francisco International airport and changed planes to reach Sonoma County airport in Santa Rosa. From there, they were picked up and driven in vans for the remaining distance to Mendocino through Cloverdale and Booneville, a severely winding and nauseating journey for many first-time visitors. Fortunately, the destination is worth any temporary discomfort.

Murder, She Wrote aired for twelve seasons, from 1984 to 1996, and remains one of the most beloved and enduring television series of all time. The show is a classic whodunit, with Angela Lansbury playing the role of Jessica Fletcher, an amateur sleuth and mystery writer who always manages to solve the crime. The show's popularity is due in large part to Angela's captivating performance as the curious author, knitting intelligence, wit, and charm together to create an instant fan-favorite character. "Deadly Lady," the first episode after the pilot in season one, was shot in Mendocino and originally broadcast on October 7, 1984. Through overcast skies and an unusual "hurricane this far north," the town sparkles.

To transform Mendocino into Cabot Cove, the show's art department didn't need to do much to create the look and feel of a New England town with traditional clapboard houses and white picket fences. Although it was a fictional place, Cabot Cove felt both timeless and characteristically American, helping to bring the show's drama to life. The Hill House, however, was, and is, a real hotel so the producers kept the name and changed the sign out front. Barbara Reed and her husband, Monte, owned the Hill House when *Murder, She Wrote* was filmed in Mendocino. In 1980, during the first phase of building the hotel on their previously undeveloped land, the Reeds received a coveted design award from the California Coastal Commission.

The couple's vision was to provide travelers with up-to-date amenities—including telephones in each room—with an ambiance to match the town's historical Victorian charm. They completed construction and opened for business in 1983. As innkeepers, they got to know many of the production's principals who stayed at the Hill House while they were in town for filming. The lobby, reception area, guest rooms, gardens, and exteriors around the hotel are also featured in scenes. And, lucky for us, Barbara had special access to the interesting stars and characters who were always happy to pose for her snaps.

Over its incredible 264-episode run, only ten episodes were filmed in Mendocino. Many other shows included stock footage from the village and the surrounding area. My mother, Toni Lemos, served as Mendocino County Film Coordinator for decades and worked closely with *Murder's* production team to ensure they had all the resources they needed to create a successful show. She provided a wealth of knowledge and contacts, assisting with background casting, location scouting, filming permits, and hiring local crew. As a darling twenty-five-year-old, Toni broke into showbiz in 1943 after being cast as the on-camera stand-in for leading actress Joan Fontaine in *Frenchman's Creek*, which was filmed in part on her parents' property in Little River, about two miles south of Mendocino. From that point on, including raising seven of us, Mom's efforts helped make our coastal scene a top choice for film and television productions, bringing significant economic benefits to the area.

I was living in Los Angeles during most of the years *Murder, She Wrote* was filming on the coast. I would often tune into the show when I needed an instant dose of home, plus I enjoy a good murder mystery. In 1987, the producers of *Overboard* picked the Mendocino area for their story's backdrop and I returned to work as a production secretary on that movie, happily discovering that many locals were knowledgeable about filmmaking thanks to working on *Murder*. In all, the town's abundance of filming locations and experienced crews made Mendocino an attractive choice for production teams during these years.

Murder, She Wrote's regular CBS airing on Sunday nights became a tradition in many households. Produced and distributed by Universal Television, the show had a high budget for its time. Some sources estimate that the cost per episode was between one and one-and-a-half million dollars, which was significantly higher than the average cost for a television show in the 1980s and early 1990s. It's easy to see where the money went: the show had high-quality production values, impressive guest stars, the very best locations, and a signature musical score. There were likely hundreds, if not thousands, of cast and crew members involved in the production of the show over its long run.

While most of the scripts for *Murder, She Wrote* were original, some episodes were based on preexisting stories or novels. Additionally, some featured adaptations of classic stories, such as *The Monkey's Paw* or *The Tell-Tale Heart*. In nearly every episode, the killer is identified and caught by the end. However, there were a few shows where the murderer was not caught or the resolution was left ambiguous. The show's writers and producers were remarkable when it came to crafting intricate mysteries, often featuring several potential suspects with plausible motives. But, for the most part, scripts were known for their formulaic approach with a focus on providing satisfying endings for fans. Guessing became great fun with winners getting bragging rights.

While *Murder, She Wrote* is primarily known for entertaining and engaging mysteries, the show also occasionally tackled social and political issues in its storylines. Such episodes tried to raise awareness of these problems and encourage viewers to think critically about social struggles and their impact on individuals and communities. "Reflections of the Mind" (S2, E6), tackles the topic of mental illness with its portrayal of a sympathetic character who suffers from schizophrenia. In "Death Takes a Dive" (S3, E16), Jessica investigates the murder of a gay boxer who is forced to hide his sexuality to maintain his career. "The Last Free Man" is a reunion movie for television that focuses on discrimination in the South. The story, starring Michael Jace, is about a man wrongly convicted of a crime because of his race.

There were so many notable guest stars throughout the show's twelve-season run, it's amazing to review the names. Did you know George Clooney is on the list? Along with the actors included in this book, other memorable guest stars of the show include Cybill Shepherd, Ernest Borgnine, George Segal, Janet Leigh, Jerry Orbach, Martin Landau, Mickey Rooney, Neil Patrick Harris, and Shirley Jones. It was important to Angela to include actors who were in the later stages of their careers. Many were seasoned players who came up in the industry with her, too. On the pages that follow, you'll see some who came to town to act with her. There is also a call sheet from a show, a list of episodes filmed in town, resources to find reruns, and a map of buildings in Mendocino transformed for Cabot Cove.

After Angela's passing in Los Angeles on October 11, 2022, I gained a deeper appreciation for her approach to her craft. With a career spanning some seven decades, her credits stack high with countless films, television shows, stage productions, and industry awards. But perhaps her most iconic role was that of Jessica Fletcher. It was this portrayal that highlighted Angela's enormous talent and charisma and the part that made her a household name.

To be sure, *Murder, She Wrote* is a classic and I imagine it will remain that way for a long time. A case in point is *Derry Girls*, a British teen sitcom that premiered in January 2018. The show is set in Northern Ireland in the 1990s. In one scene, the teens insist they can't change their Sunday night plans because they'll miss *Murder, She Wrote*. To emphasize their obsession, a large poster of Jessica is tacked to the wall of one girl's bedroom.

Over the course of the show's run, Angela received numerous accolades for her performance, including four Golden Globe Awards for Best Actress in a Television Series Drama and twelve Emmy nominations for Outstanding Lead Actress in a Drama Series. Angela was quoted in an interview with *The Guardian* in 2014 saying, "Jessica Fletcher was very real to me, and she continues to be. She was an extraordinary woman, and I will always be grateful for the opportunity to play her."

And Barbara and I are grateful Angela and Jessica became a part of Mendocino along the way.

—Jain Lemos

My husband, Monte Reed, and I were thrilled to host *Murder, She Wrote* at the Hill House… and even more touched when they decided to keep our inn's name for the show.

The Hill House lobby was a frequent gathering place for our guests to relax. When filming in this space, set director Robert Wingo roped it off with a "hot set" sign to freeze everything in place between scenes.

Angela Lansbury on Lansing Street discussing a scene with William Windom as Dr. Seth Hazlett. Angela's positive words about Mendocino reflect the impact the town had on the show's cast and crew, some who returned to spend time here on their own over the years. Monte and I always enjoyed hosting them at the Hill House and, later, at our bed and breakfast property, Reed Manor, now open as the MacCallum House Suites, overlooking town and Big River Bay.

Above: Jessica Fletcher's bike is introduced as her way of navigating Cabot Cove in the opening credits of *Murder, She Wrote*, where she is seen riding on Main Street.

Left: Angela Lansbury's chair in front of the Elisha W. Blair House, used as Jessica's Cabot Cove home for the show. The iconic property, now open as the Blair House Inn where you can enjoy a stay yourself, sits on the corner of Little Lake and Ford Streets.

Claude Akins, in front of the Hill House, cast as Captain Ethan Cragg in "Deadly Lady" (S1, E1), the first episode after the pilot, "The Murder of Sherlock Holmes." Claude was in four episodes of *Murder, She Wrote* and he appeared in more than 180 films and television shows throughout his career. He was also a fan favorite in his role as Sheriff Lobo in *The Dukes of Hazzard* series.

ON LOCATION IN MENDOCINO WITH *MURDER, SHE WROTE* 17

Ron Masak, as Sheriff Mort Metzger, practices his draw with a prop pistol in front of Jessica Fletcher's house on Little Lake and Ford Streets. The bumbling and often inept lawman of Cabot Cove was one of the show's most recurring characters. Ron was about forty-nine when he was cast for the role and he appeared in forty-one episodes.

18 MEMORIES OF CABOT COVE

Above: Filming on Main Street near the former Zacha's Bay Window Gallery, owned by local art scene pioneer Bill Zacha.

Left Top: The exterior of Saint Anthony's Catholic Church on Lansing and Palette Drive was transformed into Cobb's Mortuary. Greenskeepers brought in fresh flowers to add color to the scene. Robert Beecher (not pictured) was cast as undertaker Elias Cobb for "Deadly Lady" (S1, E1).

Left Bottom: The prop department created a display of newspapers for the lobby of the Hill House. The paper's front page headline reads, "Cosmetics Magnate Dies in Accidental Drowning," to further the story in "Deadly Lady." The sign indicates hotel guests can buy a copy of the *Cabot Cove Express* for twenty-five cents. It's another mystery that the last issue is the *Cabot Cove Tribune*.

Above: The exterior of Crown Hall on Ukiah and Kasten Streets was used as the Cabot Cove Public Library.

Right: Toni Lemos, Mendocino County Film Coordinator, waiting between scenes on Main Street with the legendary Chuck Connors, cast as FBI agent Fred Keller in the episode "Joshua Peabody Died Here... Possibly" (S2, E2). Toni loved representing our town. When anyone would ask me, "How do I get in the show?" I loved saying, "Go see Toni." She often used Crown Hall for casting sessions and other movie-making production meetings.

Above Left: Betsy Palmer appeared as Lila Norris in "Sticks and Stones" (S2, E10), when Cabot Cove is flooded with poison pen letters. She was best known for her role as the murderous Pamela Voorhees in the 1980 horror movie, *Friday the 13th*.

Above Right: Evelyn Keyes was also in "Sticks and Stones" cast as Edna. She was a well-known actress during Hollywood's Golden Age, and appeared in a few classic films, including *Gone with the Wind*, *Here Comes Mr. Jordan*, and *The Jolson Story*.

Right: Angela on her bicycle, looking very much like Jessica Fletcher.

The always amusing Leslie Nielsen in front of Patterson's Pub on Lansing Street. He arrived in Mendocino to appear in "Dead Man's Gold" (S3, E6). Cast as David Everett, the plot involves some treasure hunters who come to Cabot Cove looking for sunken riches off the coast. Leslie is perhaps best known for his comedic roles in *Airplane!* and *The Naked Gun* film series.

Tom Bosley rehearsing in front of Patterson's Pub on Lansing Street for "Dead Man's Gold" (S3, E6). Tom played the recurring role of Sheriff Amos Tupper. He first appeared on the show in 1984 and went on to make a total of eighteen appearances during the run. Of course, we also think of him as Howard Cunningham, the father of Richie and Joanie, in *Happy Days*.

Above: Chad Everett first guest-starred in "Obituary for a Dead Anchor" (S3, E9) and went on to appear in three other episodes during the show's run. His signature role was that of Dr. Joe Gannon on *Medical Center*.

Left: Savings Bank of Mendocino County on Lansing Street, originally a Masonic lodge, became the Cabot Cove Courthouse.

Above: William Windom and Monte play chess in the Hill House lobby, a favorite challenge for them. William appeared in more than fifty episodes in the recurring role of Dr. Seth Hazlitt. The portraits on the wall are of actress Linda Purl, who appeared in a few episodes of *Murder*; Danny Pintauro, who was in Mendocino for *Cujo*; and Chuck Connors in *The Rifleman*.

Right: Me, with William in the Hill House lobby.

Left: The *Murder, She Wrote* series creator and writer, Peter S. Fischer, with his wife, Lucille, who became our friends, too.

LOCATION CALL SHEET
UNIVERSAL STUDIOS

Picture: "Mirror, Mirror on the Wall"
No.: 63724
Day of Shooting: 7TH
Director: WALTER GRAUMAN
Leave Time: 9A LEAVE HOTEL
Shooting Call: 10A
Date: FRIDAY APRIL 14, 1989

PAGES	SET DESCRIPTION	SC. NO.	D/N	LOCATION
1) 1/8	EXT JESSICA'S HOUSE (ESTAB) (ATMOS)	57	D-3	MENDOCINO
3) 3/8	EXT JESSICA'S HOUSE (1)	34, 35, 36	D-3	
5) 2 1/8	EXT JESSICA'S HOUSE (1,3,5, ATMOS)	59	D-3	
6) 1/8	EXT JESSICA'S HOUSE (1)	69	D-3	
2) 2-	EXT JESSICA'S HOUSE (1,5, ATMOS)	16, 17, 18	D-2	
7) 9/8	EXT JESSICA'S HOUSE (1,5)	140	D-5	
4) 1/8	EXT JESSICA'S HOUSE (1,7,8)	39	D-3	
1 4/8	EXT JESSICA'S HOUSE (1,2)	134, 135, 136	N-4	
1/8	EXT JESSICA'S HOUSE (ESTAB)	24, 26	N-2	
8 7/8	TOTAL PAGES 13 Hours Budgeted			

Advance: Sat 4/15
EXT CABOT COVE GAZETTE sc. 73, 74 (D) MENDOCINO
EXT Sheriff's Office sc. 60, 62, 101, 90, 93, 130 (D/N)
Advance: Mon 4/17
INT Wharfside Restaurant sc. 103 pt, 104 (D)
EXT Wharfside Restaurant sc. 105-109, 120 (D)
Conditions: W/D   Cover Set: INT Hill House Lobby sc. 79

No.	Cast and Bits	Part Of	Makeup	Lv. Hotel	On Set	No.	Crew	Hotel	Lv. Hotel
1.	Angela Lansbury	Jessica	9A	8:45A	10:15A	1	Director	HH	9A
2.	William Windom	Seth	5:30PM Hold			1	Prod. Mgr.	HH	9A
3.	Ron Masak	Mort	12:30p 9:15A	9A	10:15A	1	Cameraman	TW	9A
5.	Jean Simmons	Eudora	9A	8:45A	10:15A		Cameraman		
6.	Richard Anderson (new)	Lew Braken	TRAVEL TO Mendocino			1	1st Asst. Dir.	HH	8:12A
7.	Ken Howard	Hank	11:45A	2:00p	1:45p 2:30p	1	Art Dir.	HH	O/C
8.	Daniel McDonald	Bobby	11:45A	2:00p	1:45p 2:30p		Music Rep.		
9.	Shelly Fabares	Liza	TRAVEL To Mendocino			1	2nd Asst. Dir.	TW	8:12A
15.	Richard Erdman	Jonathan (P)	TRAVEL TO Los Angeles			1	Script Sup.	TW	9A
							Prod. Asst.		
						1	DGA Trainer	TW	8:12A
						1	Cam. Oper.	TW	9A
						3	Cam. Assts.	TW	8:42A
						2	Panaglide crew	TW	9A
						1	Mixer	TW	9A
						2	Sound Crew	TW	8:42A
							Sound Crew		
						1	Makeup	TW	8:12A
						1	Makeup	TW	8:12A

No.	Extras		Report To	On Set	No.	Crew	Hotel	Lv. Hotel
4	STAND INS (Hopewell, Aendt, Sinia, Parra)		LJ Hotel	9A	1	Hairdresser	TW	8:12A
6	Townsfolk (2 w/ Bikes)		LOCATION	9A	1	Hairdresser	TW	8:12A
					3	Costumers	TW	8:12A
						CLTs	TW	9A
					5	Electricians	TW	9A
						Key Grips	TW	9A
					5	Grips	TW	9A
					3	Prop Crew	TW	9A
						Special FX	TW	9A
						Greens	LOC	9A
						Painter	TW	9A
						Wrangler		
					1	1st Aid	TW	9A
					2	Local 1A	LOC	9A
					1	Studio Teacher	TRAVEL TO L.A.
						CSE	TW	8:42A

	Transportation				Dept.	Special Notes
3	Car	Mort's car	Car carrier			
	Car	Seth's car	CC-const.			
	Car	Eudora's car	CC - Set dress		Camera	23-460 mm Lens
	Car	Titan crane	Hank's car		Props	Morning paper, suitcase & Attache case, Bag of Groceries, Gardening tools, Wicker Basket w/ apples
	Stretchout	Motorhome				
1	Bus (41 poss)	CC ward				
	Bus	CC MU				
	Camera-Sound	Jeep				
	Prop-Ward. Trk.	MU Trailer				
	Grip-Elec. Trk.	Ward Trailer				
	Generator		No.	Meals	Ready	
	Utility Trk. (overload)		90	Lunch (Michelson's)	2:30p	
	Set Dress. Trk.			Dinners		
	Constr. Trk.					
	San Wagon (7 Rm)					

Form 2492 (Rev. 9/86)

Ron Masak with Will Nye, who appeared in fifteen episodes as Deputy Floyd, in front of the Hill House in a scene for "Mirror, Mirror, On the Wall" (S5, E21–22).

Previous Pages Left: Jean Simmons appeared in season five's two-part episode, "Mirror, Mirror, On the Wall," as Jessica's old rival, Eudora McVeigh Shipton. Like Angela Lansbury, Jean was born in London; Angela in October 1925 and Jean in January 1929. Both had long, exceptional acting careers.

Above Left: Mendocino High School drama teacher Dee Lemos, with local Judy Draper, cast as background extras for an episode.

Above Right: Locals Gregory Burke and Jill Lemos played a couple checking into the hotel.

Previous Pages Right: The daily call sheet for the production's seventh day of shooting for "Mirror, Mirror, On the Wall" indicates the scenes and talent scheduled for April 14, 1989. Cast and key crew members stayed at the Hill House (HH) and other crew stayed at the Tradewinds Lodge (TW) in Fort Bragg, about eight miles north. Props are listed as: morning paper, suitcase and attaché case, bag of groceries, gardening tools, and wicker basket with apples. Part One of this episode first aired thirty days from the date of this call sheet.

Ken Howard appeared in six episodes of the show and was in Mendocino paying the part of Hank Shipton for "Mirror, Mirror, On the Wall" (S5, E21–22). Hollywood insiders will remember him as president of the Screen Actors Guild from 2009 to 2012.

Shelley Fabares was also in "Mirror, Mirror," playing the part of Liza Caspar. Fans of *The Donna Reed Show* and *Coach* will recognize her. Shelley is the niece of actress Nanette Fabray, even though Nanette played Shelley's character's mother in *Coach*.

Above: A happy crew filming in the Hill House lobby.

Left: Getting ready for a scene with Angela, Ken Howard, and Shelley Fabares at the hotel entrance.

Tom Bosley holding our dog, Moxie. Aside from film and television work, Tom was an accomplished stage performer who appeared in numerous Broadway productions throughout his career, winning a Tony Award for his performance in the musical, *Fiorello!*

Me, with a few old friends I found lying around. In an interview with the *Los Angeles Times,* Angela said this about playing Jessica Fletcher: "Our viewers love the idea of a woman who is making it on her own, who has shown that a woman of her age—60 to 65—is not over the hill and can have a fruitful, exciting life."

Wayne Rogers played the recurring role of Charlie Garrett, a private investigator and occasional love interest for Jessica. In all, he appeared in five episodes throughout the years. Fans will know him for his role as Trapper John McIntyre in *MAS*H*.

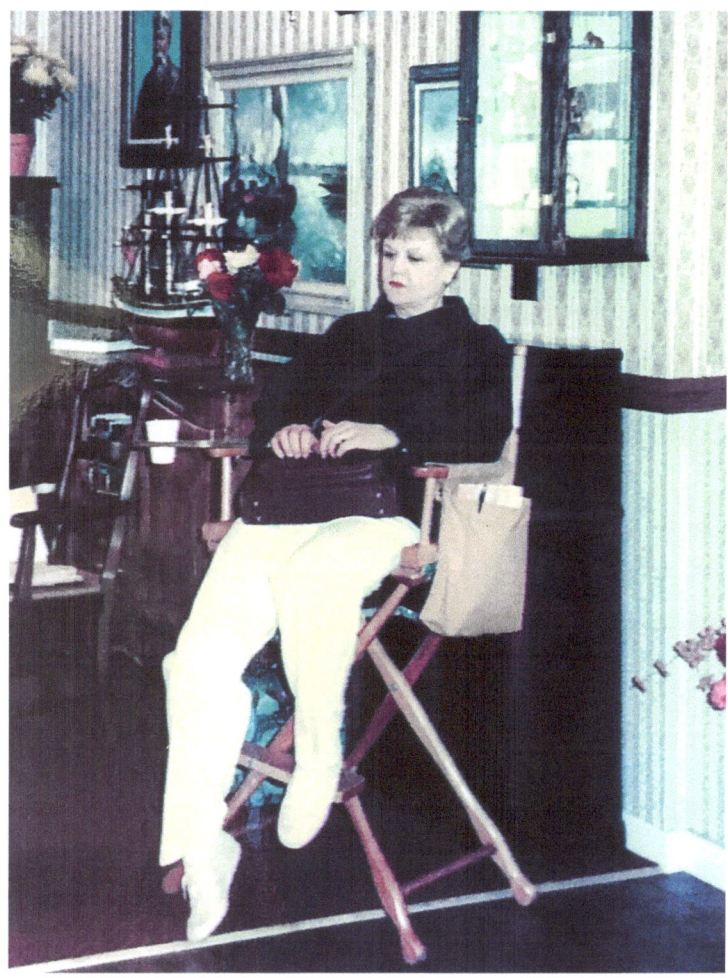

Angela takes a moment to relax between scenes in the lobby. Reflecting on the series in 2018, she told *TV Insider*, "It was a great run, and I was fortunate to be a part of it. We had wonderful guest stars, great writers, and a fantastic crew. It was truly a team effort."

Episodes Filmed in Mendocino

ONLY TEN EPISODES WERE FILMED WITH the cast and crew in Mendocino but stock footage from the show's library of the village and the surrounding area made appearances throughout *Murder, She Wrote's* twelve-year run.

1. "Deadly Lady" (Season 1, Episode 1).
   First Broadcast: October 7, 1984.
2. "Joshua Peabody Died Here… Possibly" (Season 2, Episode 2).
   First Broadcast: October 6, 1985.
3. "A Lady in the Lake" (Season 2, Episode 7).
   First Broadcast: November 10, 1985.
4. "Sticks & Stones" (Season 2, Episode 10).
   First Broadcast: December 15, 1985.
5. "Dead Man's Gold" (Season 3, Episode 6).
   First Broadcast: November 9, 1986.
6. "Obituary for a Dead Anchor" (Season 3, Episode 9).
   First Broadcast: December 7, 1986.
7. "If It's Thursday, It Must Be Beverly" (Season 4, Episode 7).
   First Broadcast: November 8, 1987.
8. "Indian Giver" (Season 4, Episode 10).
   First Broadcast: November 29, 1987.
9. "Mirror, Mirror, On the Wall: Part 1" (Season 5, Episode 21).
   First Broadcast: May 14, 1989.
10. "Mirror, Mirror, On the Wall: Part 2" (Season 5, Episode 22).
    First Broadcast: May 21, 1989.

Reruns of Murder, She Wrote

FOR NEW AND OLD FANS OF the show, here are a few places to find reruns of the series. Check your local listings or streaming platforms for more information on rerun availability. And be sure to look for the episodes that were filmed in Mendocino!

Amazon Prime Video: *Murder, She Wrote* is available to stream from Amazon, either as part of a Prime membership or for purchase.

Hallmark Movies & Mysteries: The Hallmark Channel's sister network often airs *Murder, She Wrote* reruns as part of its programming lineup.

Cozi TV: This digital broadcast network specializing in classic television shows airs *Murder, She Wrote* on a regular basis.

DVD and Blu-ray: All twelve seasons of *Murder, She Wrote* are available on DVD and Blu-ray, and can be purchased through various retailers.

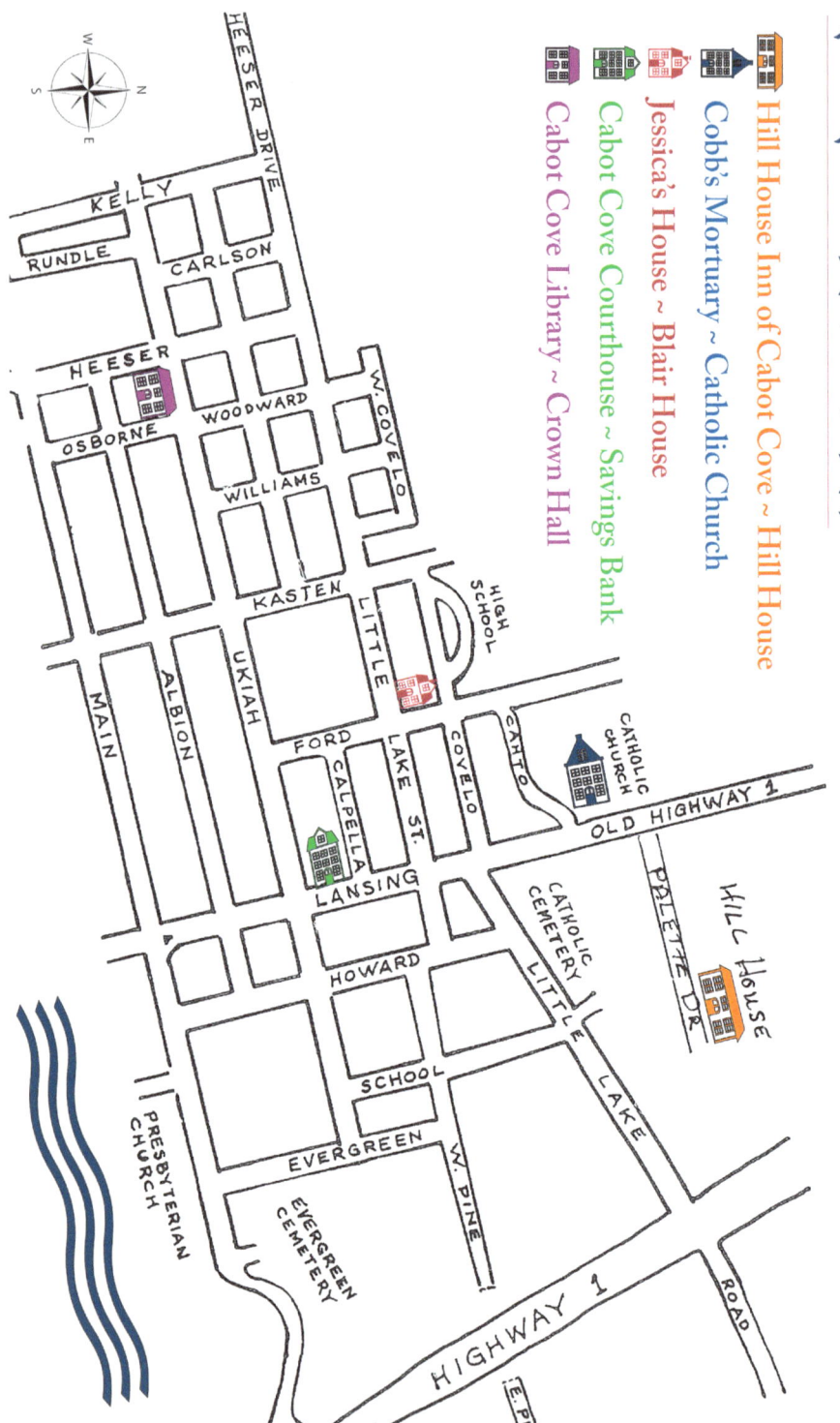

www.ingramcontent.com/pod-product-compliance
Lightning Source LLC
LaVergne TN
LVHW010030070426
835512LV00004B/55